Illustrated by
Georgene Griffin

Published by Rourke Publishing LLC
Copyright © 2002 Kidsbooks, Inc.

Printed in the USA

Rourke Publishing LLC
Vero Beach, Florida 32964
rourkepublishing.com

Griffin, Georgene
Dinosaurs / Georgene Griffin, ill.
p. cm. – (How to draw)
ISBN 1-58952-153-6

INTRODUCTION

This book will teach you how to draw many different types of dinosaurs. Some are more difficult to draw than others, but if you follow along, step by step, then (most importantly!) practice on your own, you'll soon be able to draw all the dinosaurs in this book. You will also learn the methods for drawing anything you want by breaking it down into basic shapes.

The most basic and commonly used shape is the oval. There are many variations of ovals—some are small and round, others are long and flat, and many are in between.

Most of the figures in this book begin with some kind of oval. Then, other ovals, shapes, and lines are added to form the basic dinosaur outline.

Most times a free-form oval is used, like the ones pictured below. In addition to ovals, variations of other basic shapes, such as circles, squares, rectangles, triangles, and simple lines are used to connect the shapes. Using these basic shapes will help you start your drawing.

Some basic oval shapes:

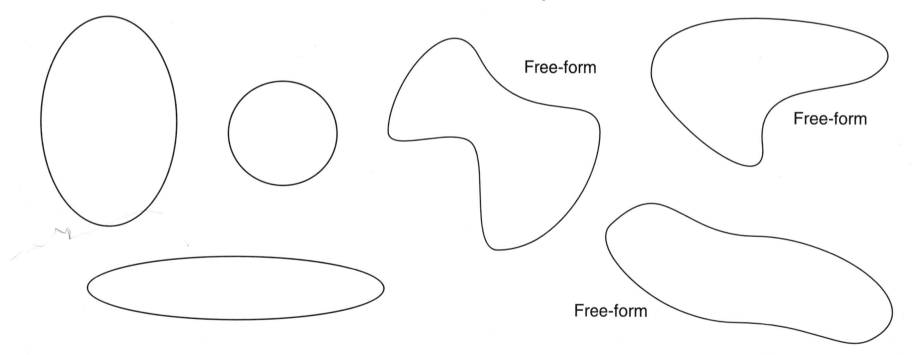

Free-form

Free-form

Free-form

SUPPLIES

Soft Pencils (#2 or softer)
Soft Eraser
Drawing Pad
Fine-Line Markers
Colored Pencils, Markers, or Crayons

HELPFUL HINTS

1. Following steps 1 and 2 carefully will make the final steps easier. The first two steps create a solid foundation of the figure—much like a builder who must first construct a foundation before building the rest of the house. Next comes the fun part—creating the smooth, clean outline drawing of the animal, and adding all the finishing touches, details, shading, and color.

2. Always keep your pencil lines light and soft. These "guidelines" will be easier to erase when you no longer need them.

3. Don't be afraid to erase. It usually takes a lot of drawing and erasing before you will be satisfied with the way your drawing looks.

4. Add details, shading, and all the finishing touches after you have blended and refined all the shapes and your figure is complete.

5. Remember: Practice Makes Perfect. Don't be discouraged if you can't get the hang of it right away. Just keep drawing and erasing until you do.

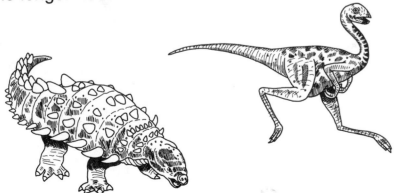

HOW TO START

Look at the finished drawing below. Study it. Then study the steps it took to get to the final drawing. Notice where the shapes overlap and where they intersect. Is the eye over the corner of the mouth or behind it? Look for relationships among the shapes.

1. Draw the main shape first—usually the largest. In this case it is a large, free-form oval for the body. Then draw an oval for the head and connect it to the body, forming the neck. Using basic shapes add arms and claws.

2. Carve out the dinosaur's mouth. Sketch additional basic shapes for the legs and tail.

3. Blend and refine the shapes into a smooth outline of the dinosaur's body. Add the sharp teeth. Keep erasing and drawing until you feel it's just right. (The dotted lines indicate that they will be erased in step 3.)

Tip: Dotted lines indicate that they will be erased in following steps.

4. Add lots of lines for shading and skin texture. Or you may color your drawing with colored pencils, markers, or crayons.

Sometimes it's helpful to start by first tracing the final drawing. Once you understand the relationships of the shapes and parts within the final drawing, it will be easier to do it yourself from scratch.

Remember: It's *not* important to get it perfect. It *is* important for you to be happy with your work!

Erasing Tips
• Once you have completed the line drawing (usually after step #2), erase your guidelines. Then proceed to add details, shading and/or coloring your drawing.
• Using a permanent, fine-line marker over your pencil guidelines will make it easier to erase the pencil lines.
• A very soft or kneaded eraser will erase the pencil lines without smudging the drawing or ripping the paper.

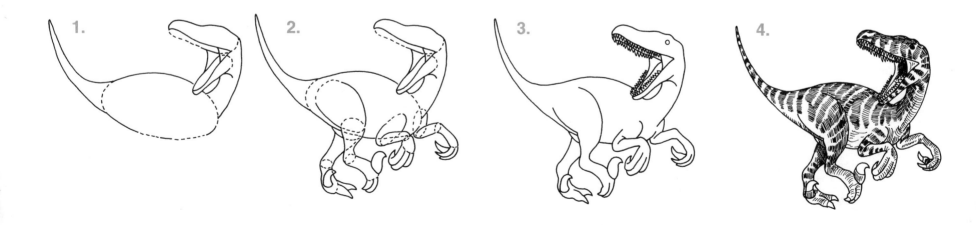

Ankylosaurus
(an-kee-luh-SAWR-us)

**Means "Stiffened Lizard" and refers to
its hard armor-plated body surface.**

1. Start your Ankylosaurus with a large oval body.
Use ovals as guidelines for its four legs. Use triangles
for its feet.

2. Next, add a long triangle for its tail with an oval on the
end. Don't forget to add some triangle shapes for "spikes"
all over its back.

4. Now finish your drawing by
adding claws to the feet, an eye,
bumpy skin, and more!

3. Erase any guidlines you don't need.
Add more bumps to its armor-plated back.

Mamenchisaurus
(mah-MEN-chee-sawr-us)

Named for the area in China, Mamenchi, where its fossils were found. Until the 1980s, Mamenchisaurus was thought to have the longest neck of any animal. It was 36 feet long.

1. Begin by lightly sketching the basic oval guideline shapes for the body and legs.

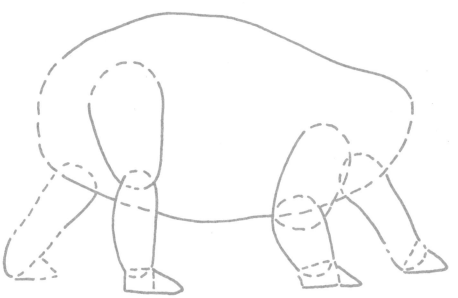

2. Draw a simple shape for the head. Connect the head to the body with two long lines, forming the neck. Add the long, curved tail.

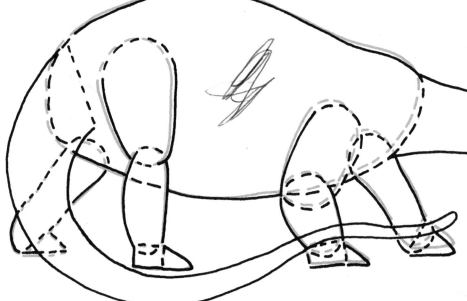

Note: Always draw your guidelines lightly in steps 1 and 2. It will be easier to erase them later.

3. Blend all the guidelines into one basic body shape. Erase any extra lines.

4. Put the finishing touches on your drawing. Adding color, shading, and skin texture will give your dinosaur a more realistic look.

Styracosaurus
(sty-RAK-uh-sawr-us)

Means "Spiked Lizard" because of the spikes on its head.

Styracosaurus was a plant eater that may have lived in herds, grazing the fields like the American buffalo of the modern world.

1. Start with a large free-form oval for the body. Add shapes for the head, lower jaw, and pointed "beak."

Note: Keep drawing and erasing until you are satisfied with the way your picture looks.

2. Next, using simple guidelines, form the legs, tail, and the triangle-shaped spikes on the dinosaur's head.

3. Add an eye with a small spike above it as shown. Combine the shapes into a smooth outline of the body. Now you're ready for the finishing touches.

4. Complete the eye and beak. Then, add lots of shading and skin details. You can even add some ground for the Styracosaurus to stomp on! For a dramatic effect, try going over the outline with a felt-tip pen.

Dilophosaurus
(dye-LO-fuh-sawr-us)

Means "Two-crested Lizard" because of the two crests on its head. Unlike other big meat-eaters, Dilophosaurus had bone joints that would have allowed it to wrinkle its nose!

1. Start by drawing two free-form ovals—one for the body and one for the head. Connect the ovals and add the tail.

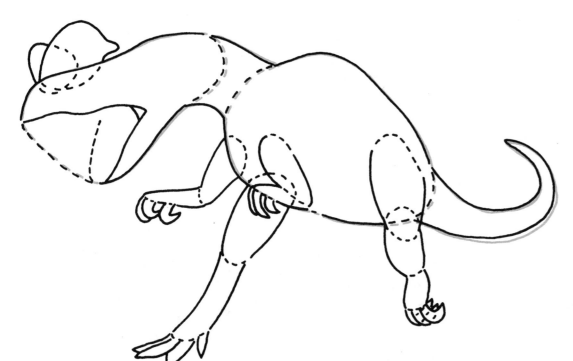

2. Next, add basic shapes for the arms, claws, legs, and feet. Draw the open mouth and add the two crests on its head.

3. Add an eye and a nostril. Blend the lines and shapes into a smooth outline of Dilophosaurus. Then add lots of pointy teeth.

Remember: Practice makes perfect. Keep drawing and erasing until you are satisfied with the way your picture looks.

4. Now add the final touches. Spots, shading, and skin wrinkles will make this dinosaur look ferociously real!

Ornithomimus
(or-nith-uh-MY-mus)

Means "Bird Imitator" because it resembled an ostrich.
Ornithomimus was very speedy and quickly ran away from danger.

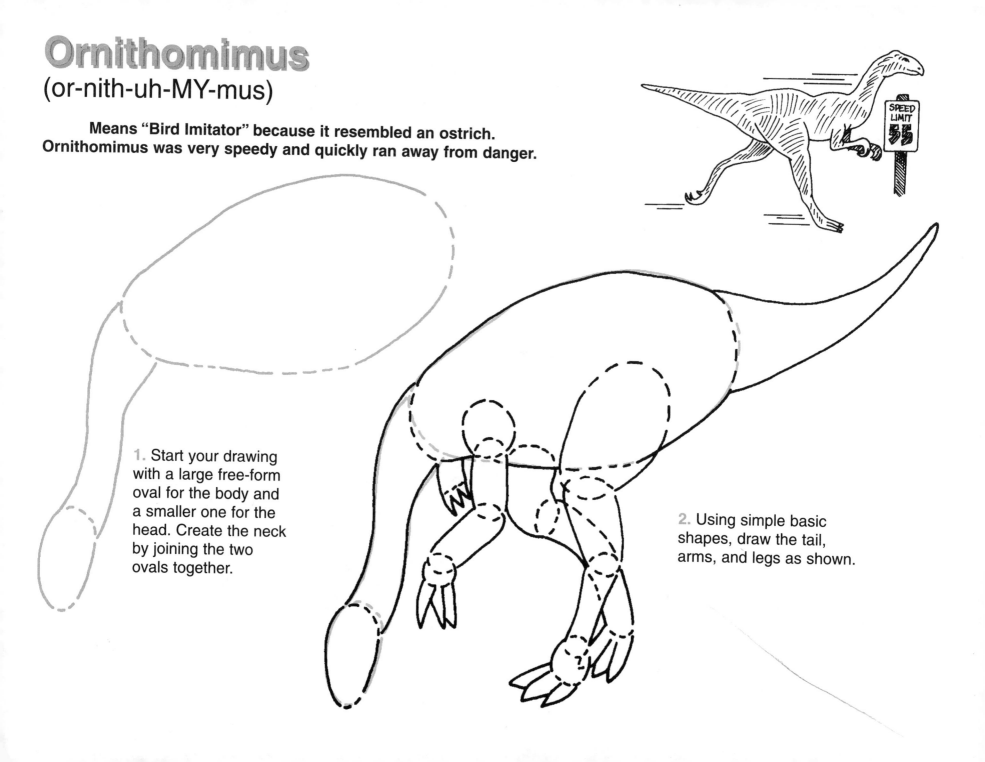

1. Start your drawing with a large free-form oval for the body and a smaller one for the head. Create the neck by joining the two ovals together.

2. Using simple basic shapes, draw the tail, arms, and legs as shown.

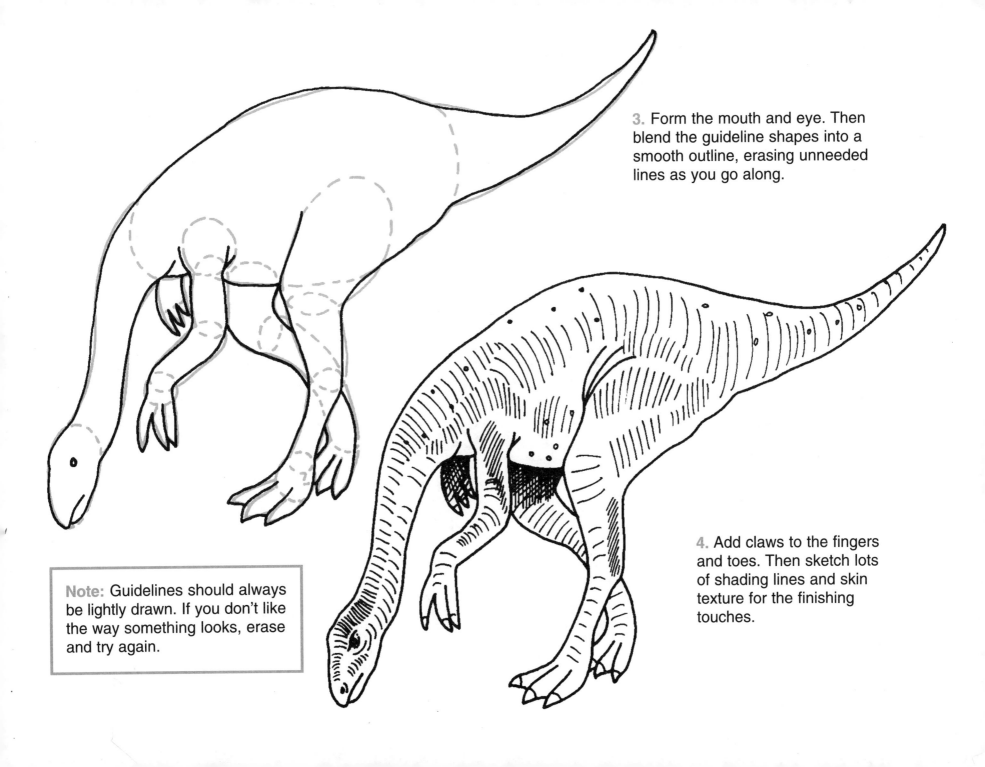

3. Form the mouth and eye. Then blend the guideline shapes into a smooth outline, erasing unneeded lines as you go along.

4. Add claws to the fingers and toes. Then sketch lots of shading lines and skin texture for the finishing touches.

Note: Guidelines should always be lightly drawn. If you don't like the way something looks, erase and try again.

Palaeoscincus

(pay-lee-o-SKINK-us)

Means "Ancient Skink" because its tooth resembles that of a modern skink. Palaeoscincus was discovered when scientists found one tooth in Montana.

Note: Steps 1 and 2 are very important. They establish the overall structure and look of your drawing. In steps 3 and 4 you are simply refining and adding details to the figure you have created in steps 1 and 2.

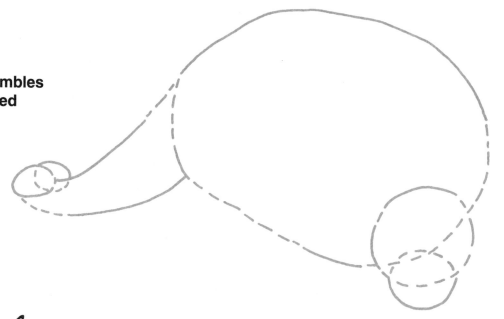

1. Begin this unique dinosaur with a large oval shape for the body and two overlapping circles for the head. Attach the tail, adding two egg-shaped ovals at the tip.

2. Add the legs and claws. Next, carefully add rows of triangle-shaped spikes all over the body and tail. Don't forget the four spikes protecting the head.

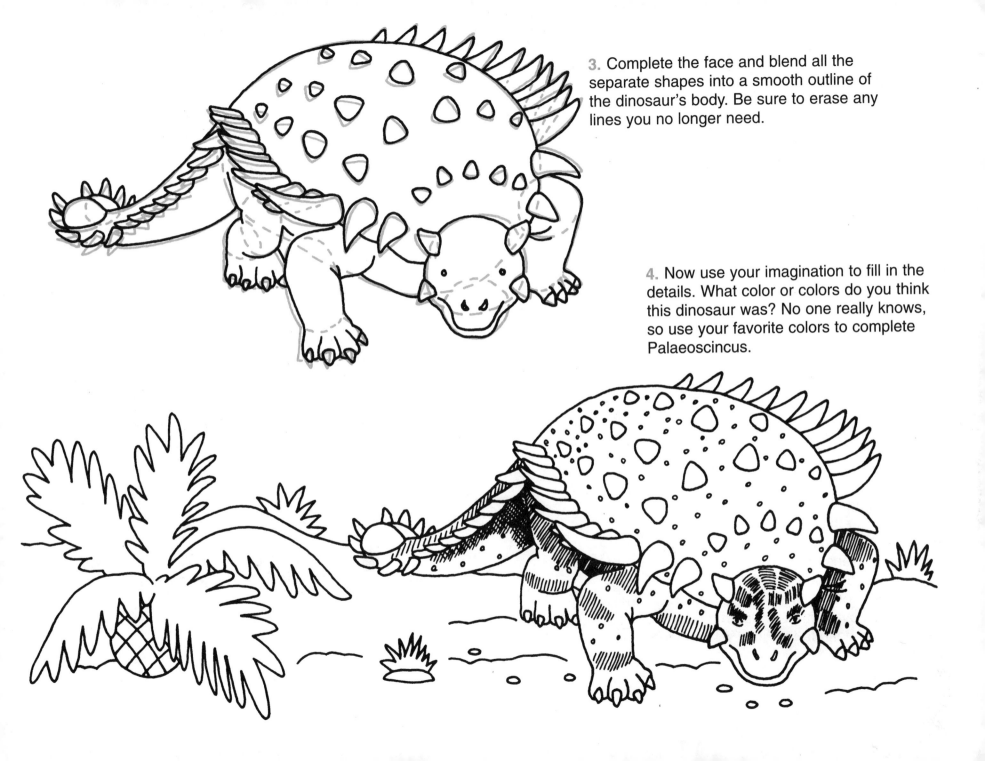

3. Complete the face and blend all the separate shapes into a smooth outline of the dinosaur's body. Be sure to erase any lines you no longer need.

4. Now use your imagination to fill in the details. What color or colors do you think this dinosaur was? No one really knows, so use your favorite colors to complete Palaeoscincus.

Diplodocus
(dih-PLOD-uh-kus)

Means "Double Beam" because of the Y-shaped vertebrae on its tail. A complete skeleton of Diplodocus measured 90 feet from head to tail. Many of this plant-eater's bones have been found in the Rocky Mountain states of North America.

1. By drawing Diplodocus at the angle shown, you can get a better sense of how gigantic this dinosaur was. Start with a very large oval for the body. Add a small circle for the chest and a small oval with a circle on top for the head. Connect the head to the body with two long lines, forming the neck.

2. Draw the rectangular-shaped legs and attach the huge, curved tail.

3. Add the eye and mouth. Then blend all your shapes into one finished outline drawing. Erase any extra lines.

4. Add details, scenery, and color. You may want to create a scene by drawing several different dinosaurs in a prehistoric setting.

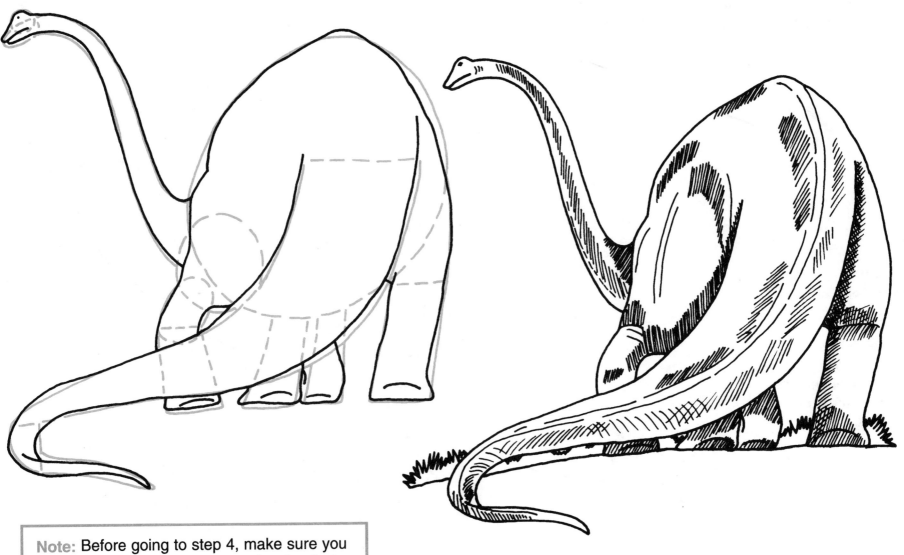

Note: Before going to step 4, make sure you are satisfied with the way your drawing looks.

Alectrosaurus
(ah-LEK-truh-sawr-us)

Means "Lizard All Alone" because it was the only Asian meat-eater of its kind when first found.

Alectrosaurus is the slimmer meat-eating cousin of fierce Tyrannosaurus.

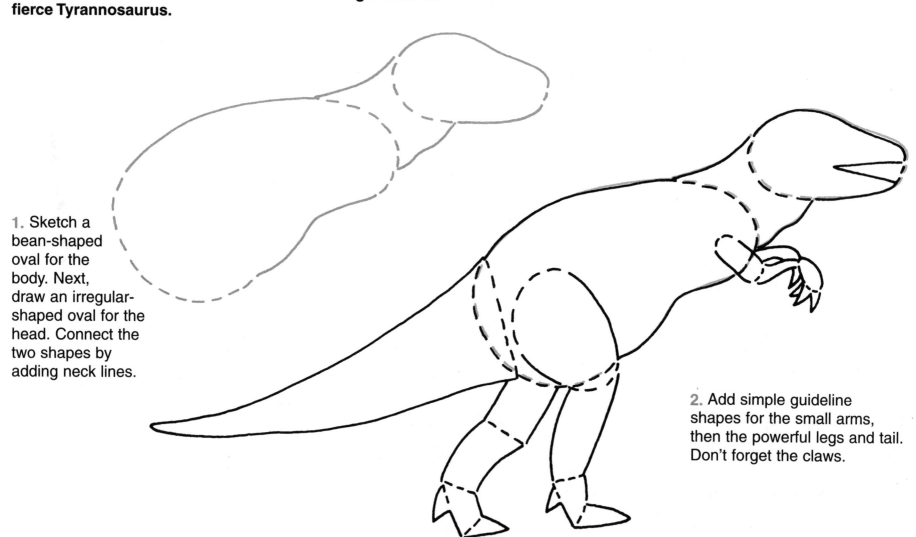

1. Sketch a bean-shaped oval for the body. Next, draw an irregular-shaped oval for the head. Connect the two shapes by adding neck lines.

2. Add simple guideline shapes for the small arms, then the powerful legs and tail. Don't forget the claws.

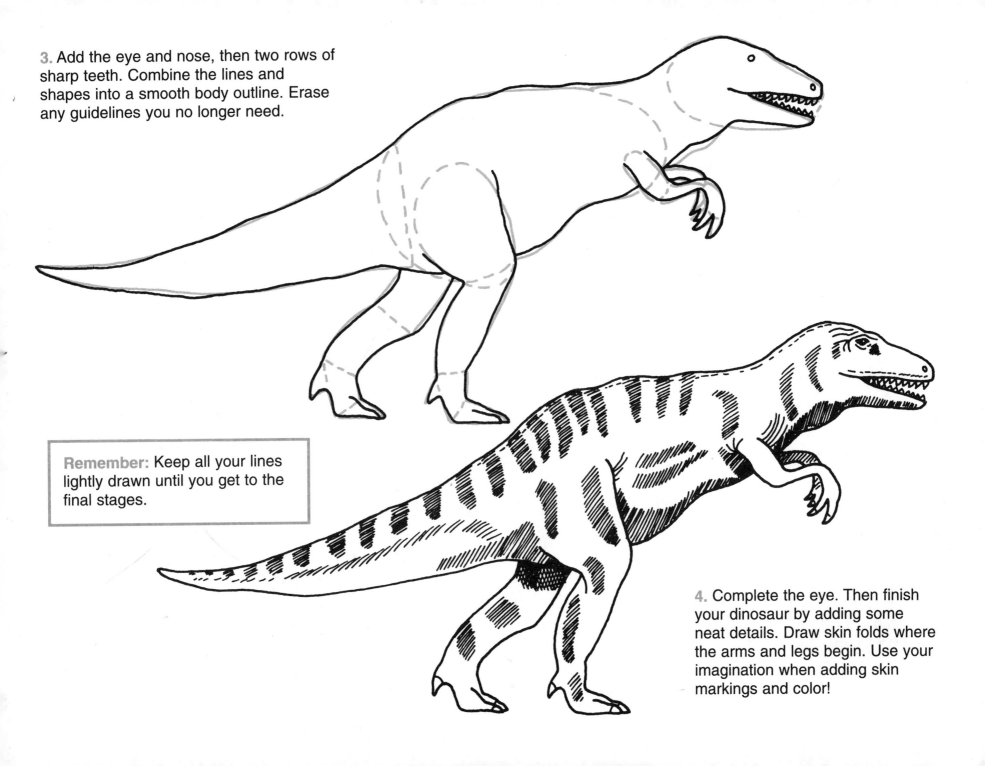

3. Add the eye and nose, then two rows of sharp teeth. Combine the lines and shapes into a smooth body outline. Erase any guidelines you no longer need.

Remember: Keep all your lines lightly drawn until you get to the final stages.

4. Complete the eye. Then finish your dinosaur by adding some neat details. Draw skin folds where the arms and legs begin. Use your imagination when adding skin markings and color!

Hylaeosaurus
(hy-LAY-ee-uh-sawr-us)

Means "Wood Lizard" because of the place in England where it was found.

Armored Hylaeosaurus lived near Wealden Lake, a body of water that formed as the continents drifted apart during the early Cretaceous period.

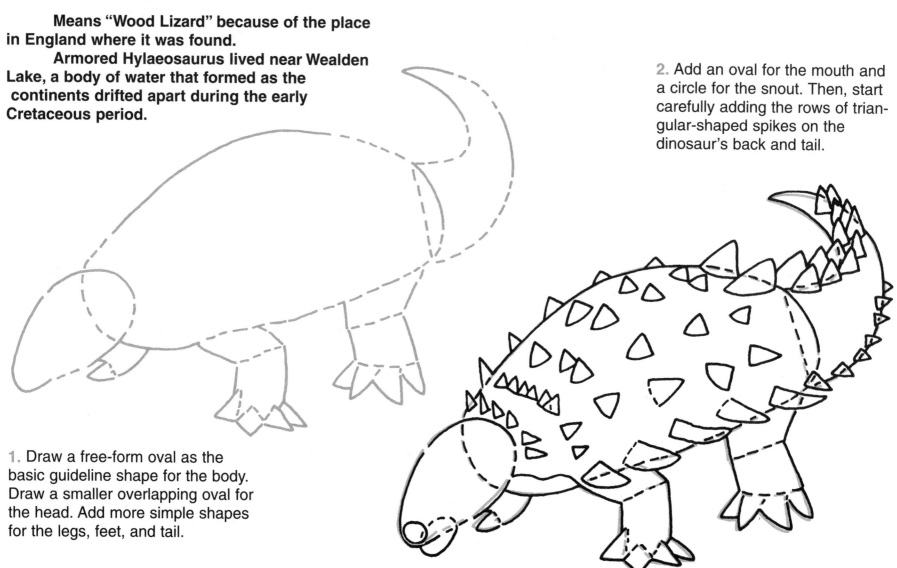

2. Add an oval for the mouth and a circle for the snout. Then, start carefully adding the rows of triangular-shaped spikes on the dinosaur's back and tail.

1. Draw a free-form oval as the basic guideline shape for the body. Draw a smaller overlapping oval for the head. Add more simple shapes for the legs, feet, and tail.

3. Add the eye, then complete the mouth and snout. Blend the shapes together, erasing unneeded lines as you go along.

4. Add teeth, plus lots of other details, wrinkles, and color to complete your Hylaeosaurus.

Hint: Breaking down complicated areas into simple shapes makes them easier to draw.

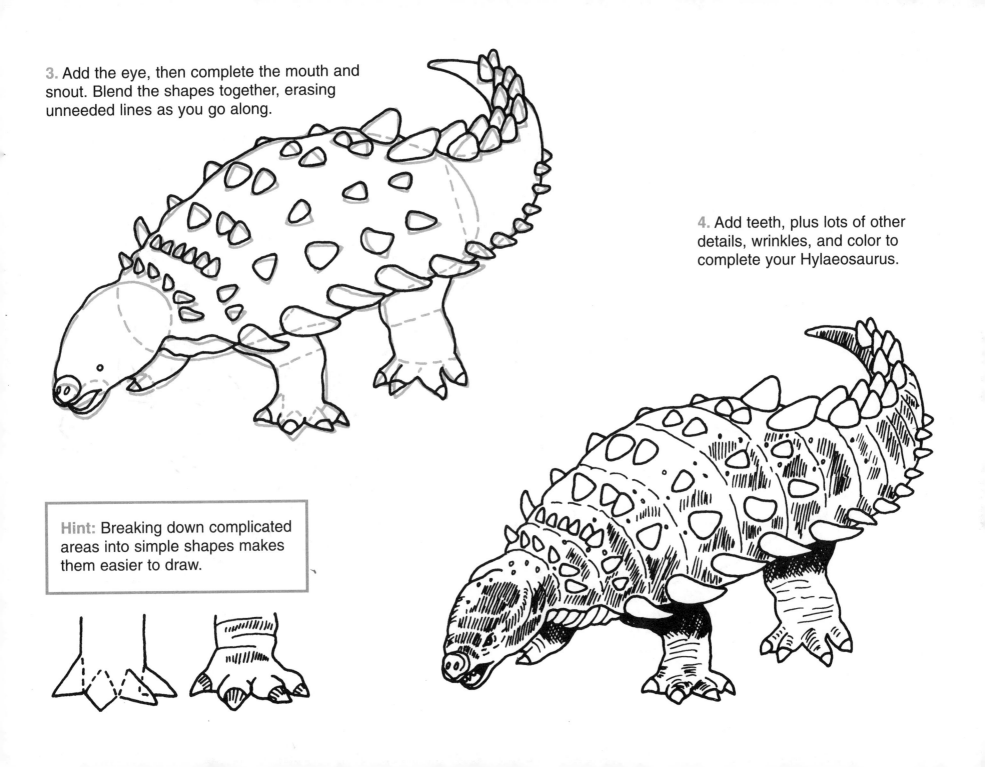

Velociraptor
(veh-loss-ih-RAP-tor)

Means "Swift Robber" due to its quickness and grasping hands.

If Velociraptor was cold-blooded, its skin would have been similar to a lizard's. If it was warm-blooded, it may have been covered with feathers or fur.

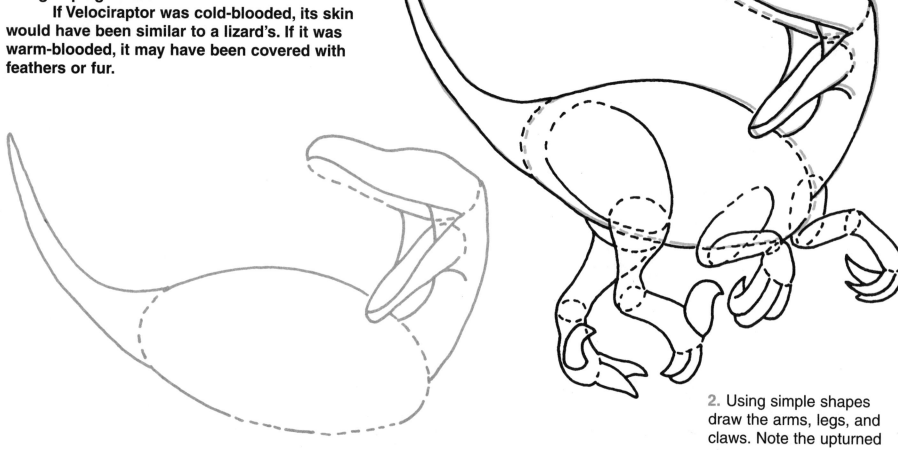

2. Using simple shapes draw the arms, legs, and claws. Note the upturned claw on the feet.

1. Lightly sketch an egg-shaped oval for the body. Next, using oval guidelines, very carefully create the upper and lower jaws and connect them to the body. Then add the tail.

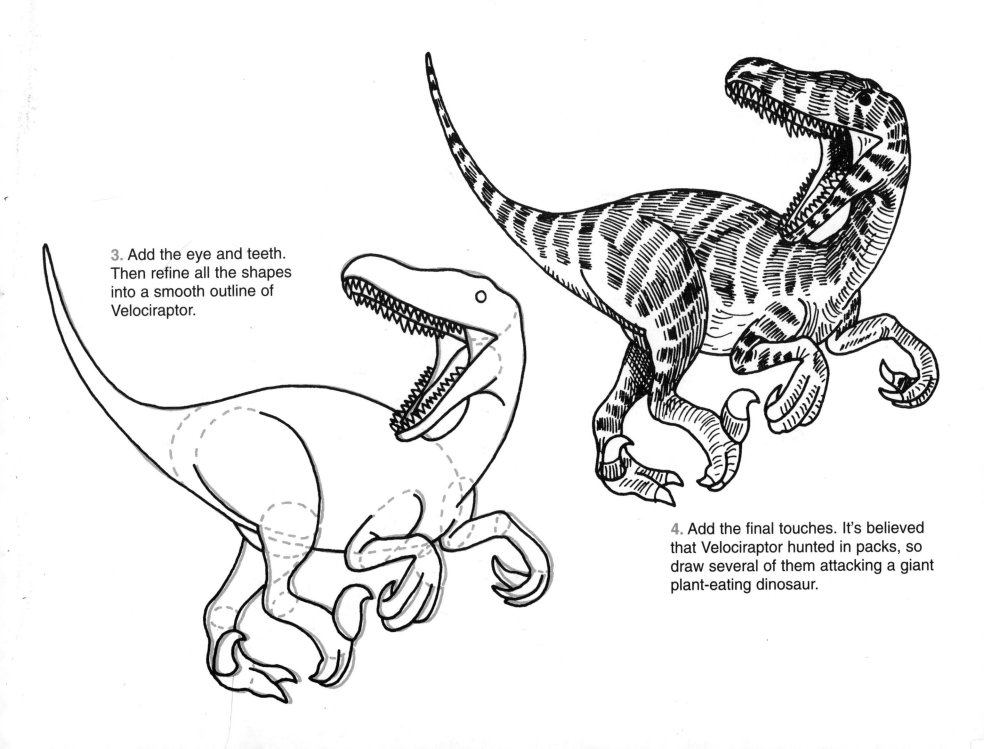

3. Add the eye and teeth. Then refine all the shapes into a smooth outline of Velociraptor.

4. Add the final touches. It's believed that Velociraptor hunted in packs, so draw several of them attacking a giant plant-eating dinosaur.

Hadrosaurus
(HAD-ruh-sawr-us)

Means "Bulky Lizard" because of its big size. In 1868, a plaster skeleton of Hadrosaurus was the first ever put on display.

1. Draw a large oval for the body and a smaller, pointy oval for the head. Connect the two ovals to form the neck. Attach a long triangle for the tail.

Note: It's usually easier to begin any drawing by sketching the largest shape first.

2. Add a line for the mouth. Next, using ovals, rectangles, and triangles, add the guideline shapes for the arms and legs.

3. Add the eye, then blend the shapes into a smooth body outline. Note the flattened snout. Keep erasing and drawing until you're satisfied with the way your dinosaur looks.

4. Create the pointy claws and complete the eye. Then add lots of shading, skin wrinkles, some color, and scenery to complete your picture.

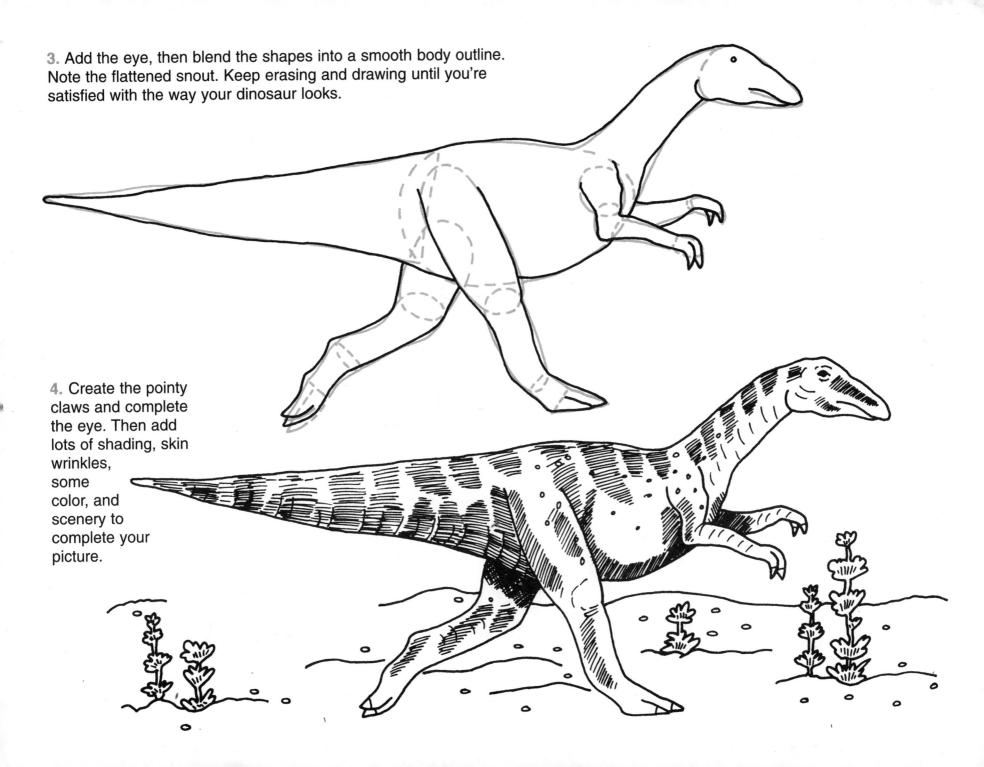

Ceratosaurus

(sair-AT-o-sawr-us)

Means "Horned Lizard" because of the horn behind its nose. Meat-eating Ceratosaurus was found at the scene of a crime in Wyoming! Its broken teeth were lying next to a fossil of a Camarasaurus skeleton.

2. Add the horn and open mouth to the head. Next, using basic guideline shapes, lightly draw the arms, hands, legs, and feet. Finally, add the curved tail.

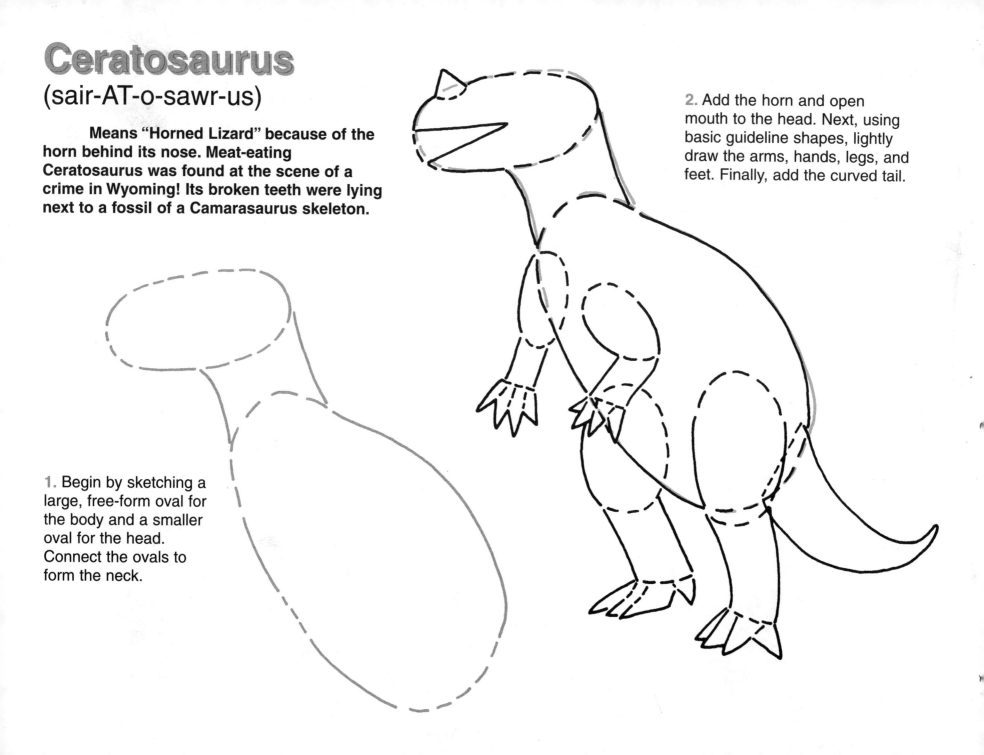

1. Begin by sketching a large, free-form oval for the body and a smaller oval for the head. Connect the ovals to form the neck.

4. Add details and shading for the finishing touches. You can outline Ceratosaurus with a black felt-tip pen or color it with your favorite colors.

3. Add the eye and sharp teeth. Then blend all the shapes together, erasing any unneeded guidelines.

Iguanodon
(ig-WAN-oh-don)

Means "Iguana Tooth" because its teeth resemble those of an iguana lizard.

About 140 million years ago, a large number of Iguanodon drowned in a lake that ran across northwest Europe. Many fossils have been found in this "Iguanodon graveyard."

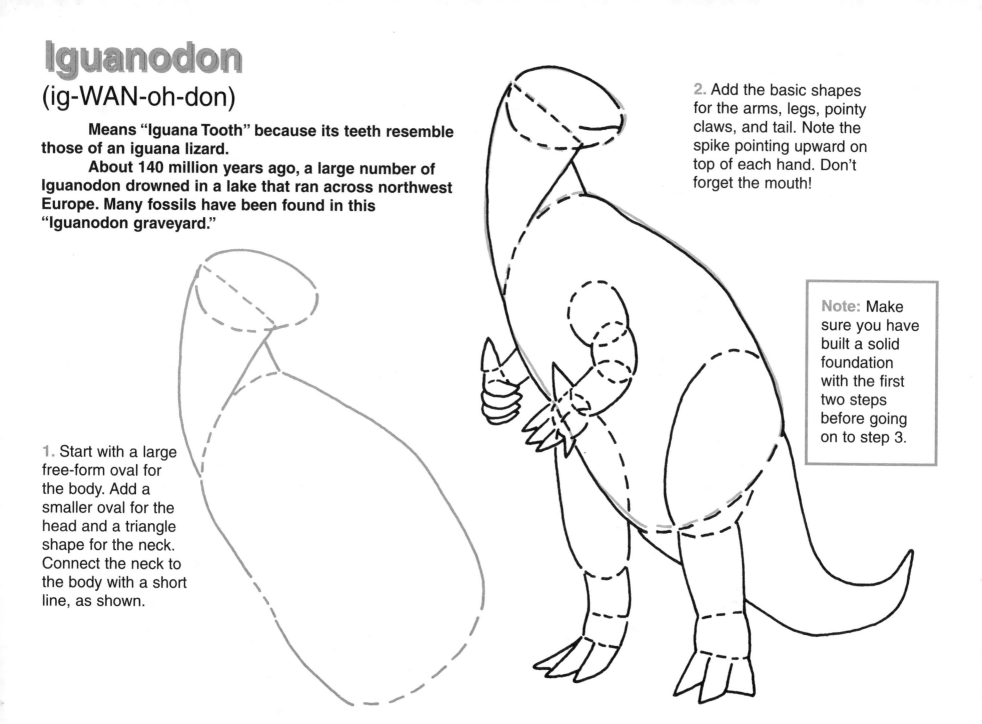

1. Start with a large free-form oval for the body. Add a smaller oval for the head and a triangle shape for the neck. Connect the neck to the body with a short line, as shown.

2. Add the basic shapes for the arms, legs, pointy claws, and tail. Note the spike pointing upward on top of each hand. Don't forget the mouth!

Note: Make sure you have built a solid foundation with the first two steps before going on to step 3.

3. Add an eye and a nostril. Erase any unneeded guidelines as you blend the shapes and lines into a smooth outline of Iguanodon.

4. Complete your drawing by adding rows of shading and skin details. Now this Iguanodon is ready to pound the prehistoric pavement!

Avimimus
(a-vee-MY-mus)

Means "Bird Mimic" due to its birdlike appearance. Some scientists believe Avimimus was similar to the modern-day roadrunner, and that it might have even had feathers!

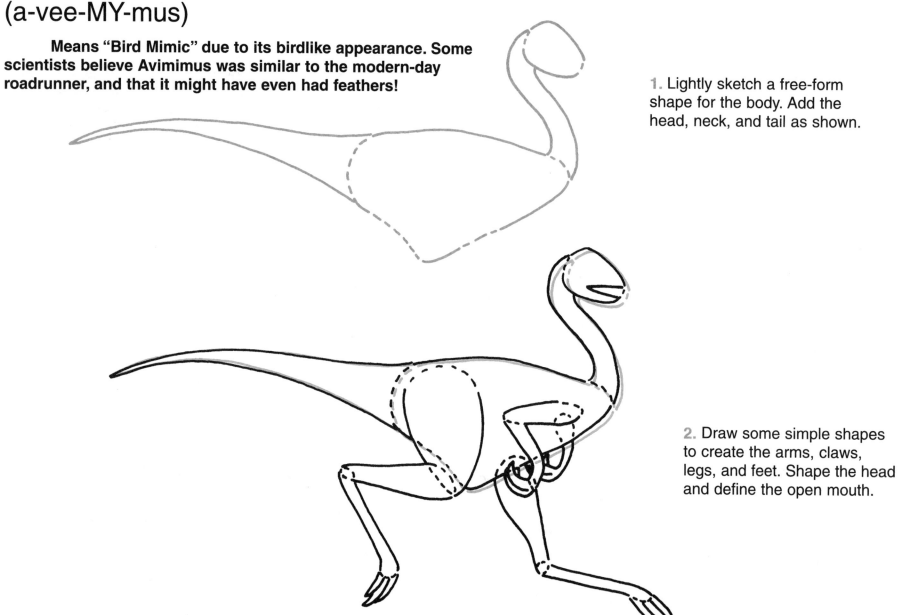

1. Lightly sketch a free-form shape for the body. Add the head, neck, and tail as shown.

2. Draw some simple shapes to create the arms, claws, legs, and feet. Shape the head and define the open mouth.

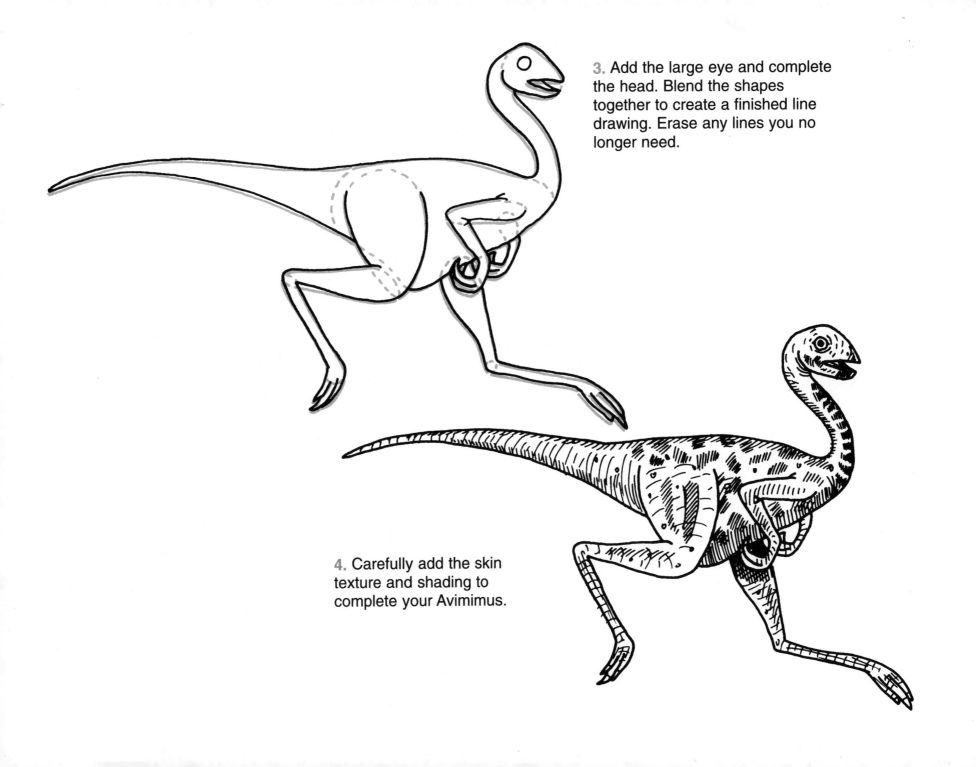

3. Add the large eye and complete the head. Blend the shapes together to create a finished line drawing. Erase any lines you no longer need.

4. Carefully add the skin texture and shading to complete your Avimimus.

Coelophysis
(see-lo-FISE-iss)

Means "Hollow Form" and refers to its hollow bones.

1. Start your drawing with basic shapes for the head, neck, body, arms, and legs.

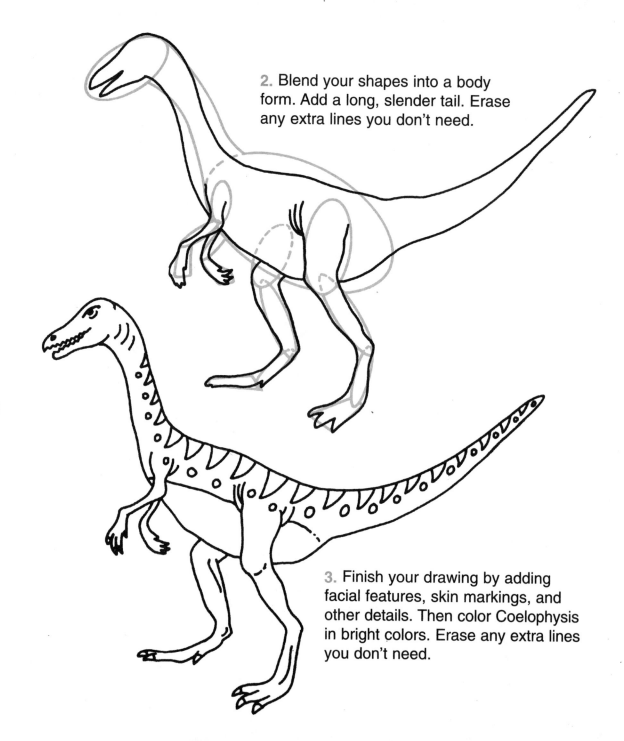

2. Blend your shapes into a body form. Add a long, slender tail. Erase any extra lines you don't need.

3. Finish your drawing by adding facial features, skin markings, and other details. Then color Coelophysis in bright colors. Erase any extra lines you don't need.